FOLDING NAPKINS

FOLDING NAPKINS

GAY MERRILL GROSS

PHOTOGRAPHY BY MICHAEL GRAND

FRIEDMAN/FAIRFAX
PUBLISHERS

A FRIEDMAN/FAIRFAX BOOK

Copyright © 1993, 1997 by Michael Friedman Publishing Group, Inc.

ISBN 1-56799-622-1

Editor: Sharon Kalman
Art Director: Jeff Batzli
Designer: Lynne Yeamans
Photography Editor: Christopher C. Bain
Illustrator: Steven Arcella

All photographs © Michael Grand, except where noted on page
© Tony Cenicola

Typeset by The Interface Group, Inc.
Color separations by Kwong Ming Graphicprint Co.
Printed and bound in China by Leefung-Asco Printers Ltd.

For bulk purchases and special sales, please contact:
Friedman/Fairfax Publishers
15 West 26 Street
New York, NY 10010
(212) 685-6610 FAX (212) 685-1307

Visit our website:
http://www.metrobooks.com

ACKNOWLEDGMENTS

*I wish to thank the following people for offering creative ideas
and other assistance with writing this book:*

*Rachel Katz; Laura Kruskal; Lillian Oppenheimer; Jan Polish; Rosalyn Gross;
Jacqueline and Jean-Paul Latil; Kyoko Kondo; Mark Kennedy; Ruthanne Bessman;
Kathleen Beyer; Trish Troy Truitt; Carol Ann Wilk; Sharon Kalman, Sharyn Rosart, and
the staff at the Michael Friedman Publishing Group; Lynne Yeamans, designer and stylist;
photographer Michael Grand; and The Friends of The Origami Center of America.*

*To the best of my knowledge, all the napkin folds in this book,
unless otherwise credited, are traditional designs.*

*The publisher would like to thank the following people for supplying the
items seen in the photographs: most napkins were supplied by "Now Designs,"
which can be seen at Remington Freeman Ltd., New York, NY; the silverware
was provided by Yamazaki Tableware Inc., 150 North St., Teterboro, NJ 07608;
the china was graciously donated by Fitz and Floyd, Inc., Dallas, Texas.*

CONTENTS

INTRODUCTION

Just as a necktie or scarf adds color and style to an outfit, a decoratively folded napkin really dresses up your table. Napkin folding is fun to do and is appreciated by your guests. It also allows you to be creative by choosing patterns and types of napkins and the kind of fold that will add just the right touch to your meal. Some folded patterns can be real showstoppers, while others add a more subtle note of style to your table. Some designs will make your table look very festive, while others may be very practical, helping you to carry silverware from a buffet table, serving as a placecard holder, keeping a roll warm, hiding an after-dinner mint, or doubling as a hot plate or mitt to protect your hands when passing a hot dish.

Decoratively folded napkins are almost always a conversation-starter at the table. Your guests may even have fun trying to unfold your handiwork to figure out how it was done.

Most of the napkin fold patterns here are considered traditional. You may see them adorning the tables of the finest restaurants. Others come from people at home who are creating new ways to decorate their own table. Indeed, you may use the instructions and photographs here to stimulate your own creativity and make your own patterns or variations on those already shown.

While paper napkins are more commonly used in American homes, this is not the case in many other countries. Perhaps it has to do with the fact that trees, and therefore paper for throwaway use, are not as abundant in other countries.

When cloth napkins are used on an everyday basis, as they are in many European homes, they are usually reused several times, just as you would use a face towel a few times before laundering. But how do you tell at the next meal which was your napkin after they have all been put away? A family I stayed with in Spain gives each family member a different color napkin. In France, simple envelopes were sewn out of cloth. At the end of a meal you would store the napkin you had just used in your envelope, which was embroidered with a design or your name to distinguish it from the other cloth envelopes. Another method used in France would be for everyone to fold their napkin in a different pattern before putting it away, so that at the next meal you could tell from the fold which was your napkin. This is the origin of the Hers and His napkin folds shown in this book (see pages 32 and 35).

Most designs work best when folded from cloth napkins. If you are using paper napkins, try to use large, three-ply napkins. Many designs require that your napkin be square, so look at the dimensions on the package before purchasing; many paper napkins are not perfectly square. In a pinch, you can always trim a paper napkin to the proper size.

Cloth napkins should be ironed after laundering. Also, many designs will hold their shape better when the napkin has been starched. Ideally, to avoid unwanted creases that may show on the finished design, napkins that have been starched and ironed should be stored perfectly flat until they are used. If this is not possible, then you can either re-iron them before using, or plan ahead by folding the beginning creases for the design you think you may use next (such as folded in half, thirds, or quarters), and storing them in this shape.

Cloth napkins made from polyester blend will tend to resist creases more than all-cotton or linen napkins, and may even begin to unfold themselves. Use these napkins for folds that are anchored in a glass or napkin ring, where the "spreading" effect may be desirable. Avoid using them for designs that stand on their own and require sturdy material.

SIZE OF NAPKINS

While most designs work best when folded from a large napkin (around twenty inches [51 cm] square), more intricate folds may require an even larger napkin, while simpler folds may be possible from small napkins. Experiment with what you have on hand to see what works best.

SETTING THE TABLE

Many people wait until right before their guests arrive to set the table or fold napkins. Unless you need your dining table for other purposes before eating, you may want to consider getting the table ready ahead of time. In any case, you can always prepare your napkins early in the day (or the day before) and leave them completely folded or at the step before they become three-dimensional (if a sculptured fold) and set them aside in a pile.

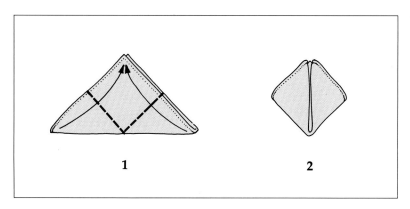

1   2

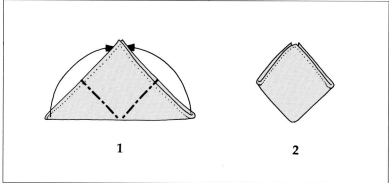

1   2

A line of dashes means to fold forward.

A line of alternating long dashes and short dashes means to fold backward.

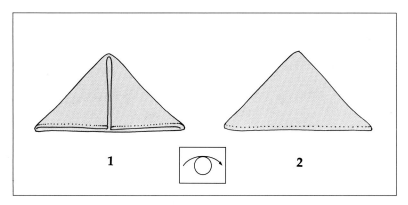

1   2

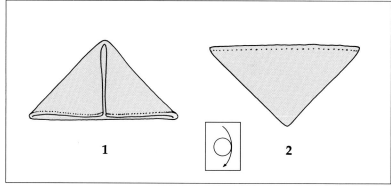

1   2

A looped arrow means to turn the model over in the direction of the arrow.

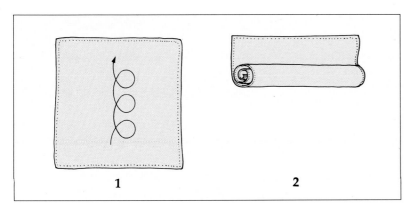

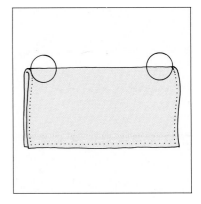

An arrow with many loops means to roll the napkin in the direction of the arrow.

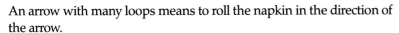

A dotted line indicates a hidden edge, or the position of a fold after it is made.

A circle means to hold the napkin here.

HOW TO FOLD A NAPKIN INTO QUARTERS

Some of the directions in this book instruct you to begin with a napkin folded into quarters. If you are using a paper napkin, this is exactly how it usually comes in the package and you are ready to begin. Otherwise, here are directions for folding into quarters:

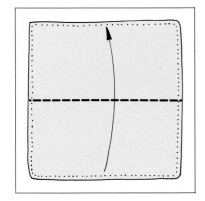

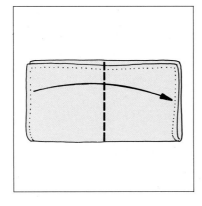

1. Fold the napkin in half.

2. Fold in half again.

3. Your napkin is now folded into quarters. One corner will have four loose corners. The beginning instruction for the fold will usually tell you where to place this corner.

CHAPTER ONE

Flat Designs

BREEZE

(Design by the author)

Create a windswept look at your table with this simple fold.
Either cloth or paper napkins can be used.

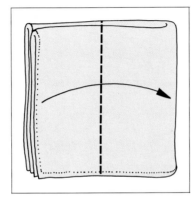

1. Begin with a napkin folded in quarters. The four free points should be at the bottom left corner. Fold the left side over to the right, folding the napkin in half.

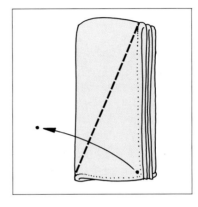

2. Lift up the first free point at the bottom right corner and fold it up and to the left as far as you can, creating a diagonal fold.

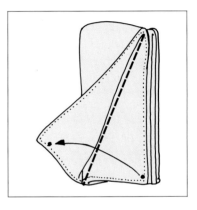

3. Repeat with the next free point at the bottom right corner, bringing it approximately one-quarter inch (.6 cm) away from the first layer folded up.

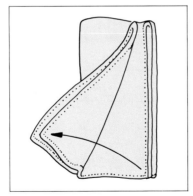

4. Repeat with the next two layers, always leaving a slight gap between layers.

5. The completed fold looks as if a strong breeze came along and blew it open.

BUN WARMER
(Adapted by the author)

Here's a novel way to present your napkins and keep each guest's bun or roll warm and fresh. Use a large cloth napkin (approximately twenty inches [51 cm]).

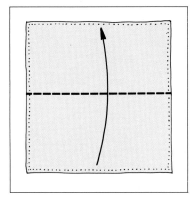

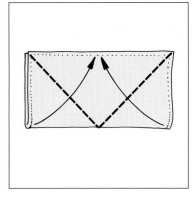

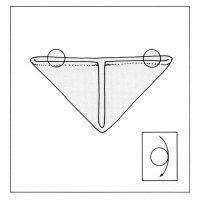

1. Begin with an open, square napkin. Fold the bottom edge up to the top edge.

2. Bring the right and left bottom points up to meet at the center of the top edge.

3. Hold the top edge of the triangle (the long edge) by the side points and flip the napkin over to the other side, so that the long edge of the triangle is now at the bottom.

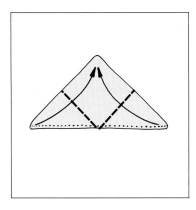

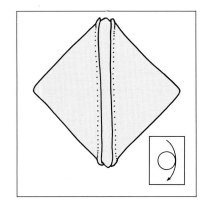

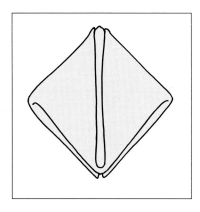

4. Bring the side points up to the top point.

5. Hold the top points and flip the napkin over again. (The top corner will now be at the bottom.)

6. Completed Bun Warmer. Slip a bun into the pocket formed by the center slit or lift up the first point at the bottom corner and hide the bun under this layer.

DECO

This attractive and simple design can be folded from a cloth or paper napkin.

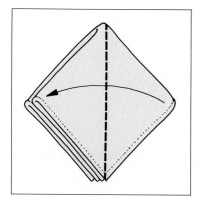 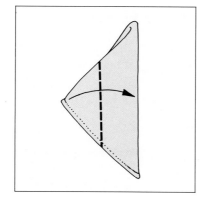 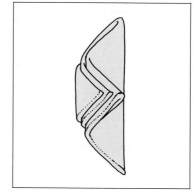

1. Begin with a napkin folded in quarters. Position the napkin so that the four free corners are pointing down and the side with two corners is on the left. (The folded edge is on the right.) Bring the right corner over to the left corner, folding the napkin in half.

2. Fold all points at the left corner to the center of the right folded edge. Slightly separate the three points you folded over so that each can be seen individually.

3. Completed Deco design.

The very elegant look of this design adds a touch of class to your table. If you wish, silverware, a flower, or a name card can be inserted into the pockets behind the bands.

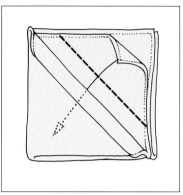

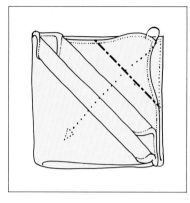

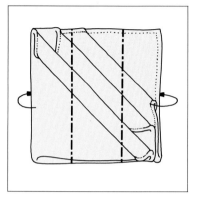

1. Begin with a napkin folded into quarters. Position the napkin so that the four free corners are at the top right. Lift the first free corner and roll it diagonally down toward the opposite corner, stopping just past midway or as far as you can comfortably roll. Flatten the roll into a narrow band.

2. Lift the band slightly and at the same time lift the next free corner at the top right. Slip the corner part way into the pocket behind the band. The folded edge should form a band that is parallel to and approximately the same width as the first band.

3. Lift the third free corner and fold it backward and behind the second band to form a third band equal in width to the first two.

4. Fold the right and left sides to the back.

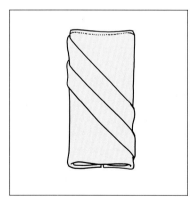

5. Completed Diagonal Stripes.

Variation: Instead of forming three bands, this fold can be made with either one or two bands.

DIAMOND IN THE SQUARE
(Contributed by Susan Kalish)

For a bold geometric effect, choose a cloth napkin in a color that
contrasts with the color of your dinnerware.

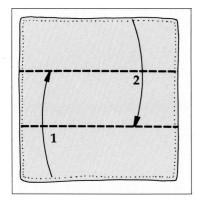

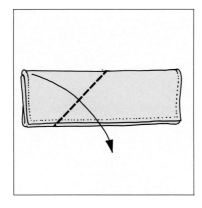

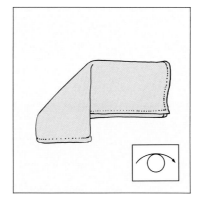

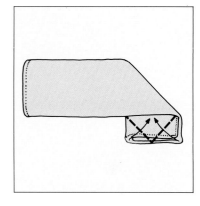

1. Begin with an open, square napkin. Fold it in thirds (as you would fold a letter). The open edge should be at the bottom.

2. Place a finger at the center of the top edge and bring the top left corner down.

3. Turn the napkin over and position it so that the slanted edge is on the right.

4. A rectangle should extend below the bottom of the right side. Fold the right and left corners of the rectangle up to the folded edge.

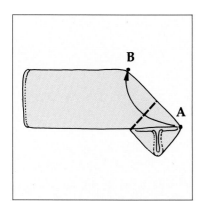

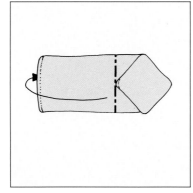

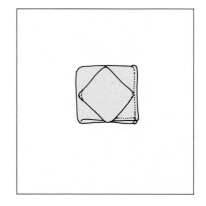

5. Fold point A up to lie on point B, creating a diamond shape at one end of the strip.

6. Fold the left edge of the strip backward so that the edge lies directly behind the right corner of the diamond.

7. Completed Diamond in the Square.

DOUBLE FLAP PURSE

(Design by the author)

This handsome fold looks distinguished draped across a plate with the flaps pointing down, like a purse, or turned sideways and placed to the left of the plate.

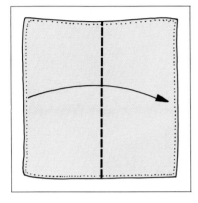

1. Begin with an open, square napkin. Fold the left side over to the right.

2. Fold the top corners down to form a point at the top.

3. Fold the bottom edge up so it covers the top point.

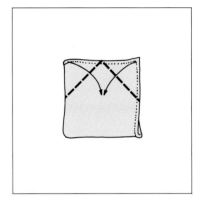

4. Fold the new top corners down to form another point that lies over the point made in step 2.

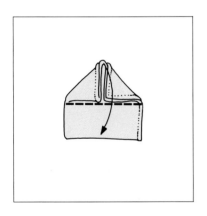

5. Fold the front point down to the bottom edge of the napkin.

6. Fold the remaining point down so that it rests slightly higher than the first.

7. Completed Double Flap Purse.

EMPEROR'S ROBE

(Design by the author)

This regal design looks best using a cloth napkin at least twenty inches (51 cm) square.

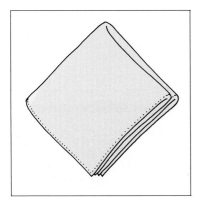

1. Fold the napkin into quarters. Place it on the table so that the four free corners are at the bottom.

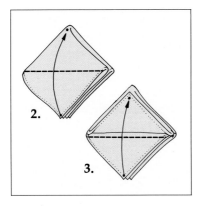

2–5. Fold up each of the bottom corners in succession, bringing each a little lower than the previous corner.

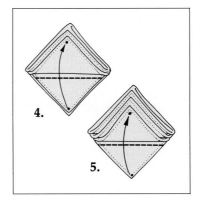

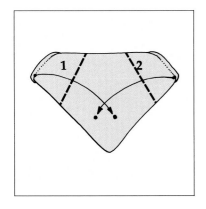

6. You should now have all the corners folded up and evenly spaced apart. Hold the napkin at the bottom edge and flip it over so that the bottom edge is now at the top.

7. Fold the side corners toward the center as shown (see drawing 8).

8. Fold the bottom point behind.

9. Completed Emperor's Robe.

H A O R I
(Design by Laura Kruskal)

*A haori is a coat worn over a kimono. With this design you can
achieve the same Oriental accent as with the Kimono fold (see page 37),
but with a much simpler folding pattern.*

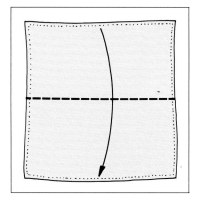

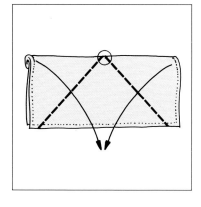

1. Begin with an open napkin. Bring the top edge down to the bottom edge.

2. Fold the top edge behind to form a hem at the back of the napkin.

3. Place a finger at the center of the top edge. Fold the top right and left corners down to meet at the center.

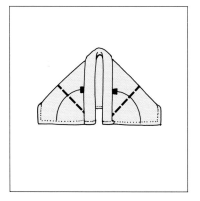

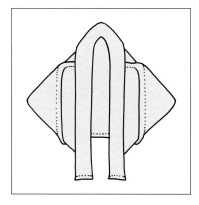

4. Fold the bottom right point up to the center and tuck the edge under the band formed by the hem. Repeat on the left side.

5. Completed Haori. If you wish, hide a mint or a message under one sleeve.

After dinner, Jacqueline Latil's grandmother would fold
her napkin into this triangular shape to differentiate it from the
grandfather's (His) napkin (see page 35).

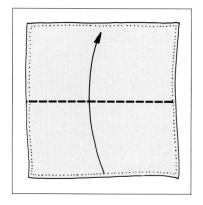

1. Begin with an open, square napkin. Fold the bottom edge up to the top edge.

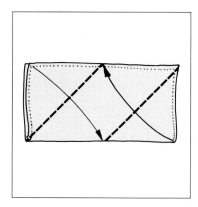

2. Fold the top left corner down to the bottom edge. Fold the bottom right corner up to the top edge.

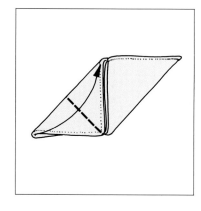

3. Fold the bottom left point up to the top.

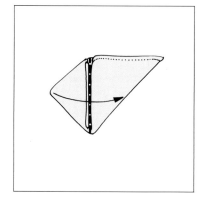

4. Fold the triangle at left over to the right.

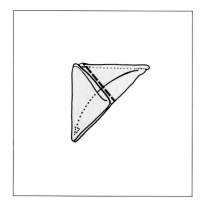

5. Notice the pocket at the center line of the large triangle. Insert the top right point into the pocket. Push it in as far as it will go.

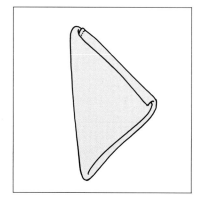

6. Leave the napkin as is, or open it at one side and round the triangle into a cone shape.

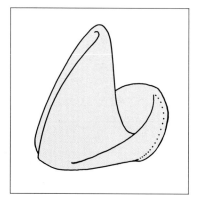

7. Then turn the bottom corner up to form a hat or sailboat that you can stand up.

When Jacqueline Latil was growing up in France, she remembers that after dinner her grandfather would fold his napkin into a rectangular shape. When the napkins were taken out of the drawer the next day, it was easy to tell which was his napkin and which was hers. • This variation on the grandfather's fold makes a neat little bag, or if you are passing a hot dish around the table, lay a couple of these out to be used as pot holders. If you are using a napkin with a printed pattern, begin with the patterned side facing up.

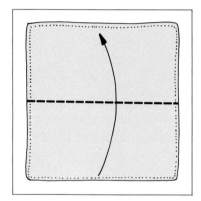 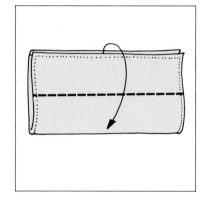 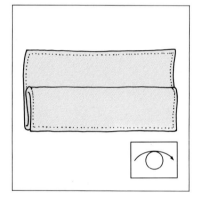 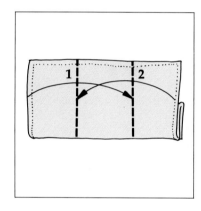

1. Begin with an open napkin. Bring the bottom edge up to the top edge.

2. There are two edges at the top of the napkin. Take the front edge only and fold it down to the bottom edge.

3. Turn the napkin over so that the folded edge remains at bottom.

4. Fold the napkin in thirds, as shown.

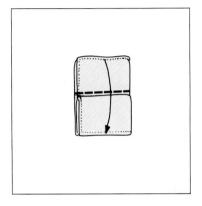

5. Fold the top edges (all layers) down to the bottom of the napkin.

6. At the top edge of the napkin is a pocket. Insert your hands into the right and left sides of the pocket, leaving your thumbs on the outside. Turn the napkin inside out (like a glove).

7. Neaten the corners of the pouch by poking your fingers down to the bottom, and the His fold is completed.

KIMONO

Based on the traditional Japanese origami kimono folded from paper, this charming design will so impress your guests that they will be reluctant to unfold it! This fold requires a little practice and a starched cotton or linen napkin.

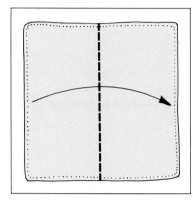

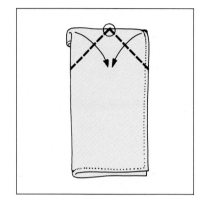

1. Begin with an open napkin. Fold it in half, from left to right, to form a rectangle.

2. Fold the top edge backward to form a small hem (approximately one inch [2.5 cm]).

3. Place a finger at the center of the top edge and fold the right and left top corners down to meet at the center, forming a triangle.

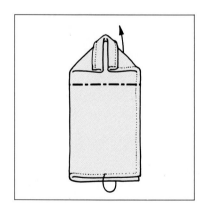

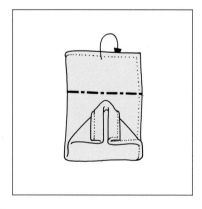

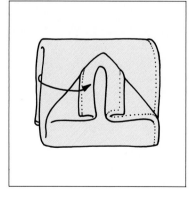

4. While holding the top triangle in place, flip the bottom edge behind and above the triangle, creating a fold slightly below the bottom of the triangle.

5. Fold the top edge behind. It should lie approximately in line with the bottom of the triangle.

6. There are two folded edges at the top of the left side. Separate these edges and fold the front layer over to almost the center of the napkin.

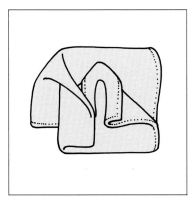

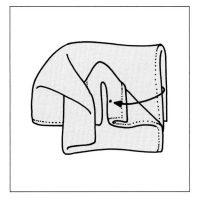

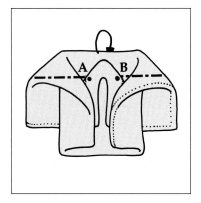

7. At the top of the separated layers is a loosely formed, irregular triangle. Flatten this triangle to appear as shown in drawing 8.

8. Repeat steps 6 and 7 on the right side.

9. Fold the top edge and part of the irregular triangles backward so that the fold you create is directly behind points A and B.

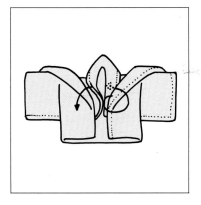

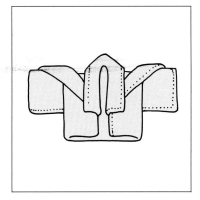

10. Lift up the right and left sides of the center hem and tuck the center edges of the kimono under them.

11. Completed Kimono.

MONOGRAM FOLD
(Contributed by Susan Kalish)

*This fold is an ideal way to show off a napkin with a monogram,
a decoration, or a lacy edge at one corner.*

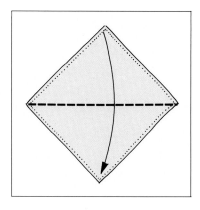

1. Begin with an open, square napkin in the shape of a diamond. The corner with the monogram or decoration should be at the bottom, on the underside of the napkin. Bring the top corner down to the bottom corner.

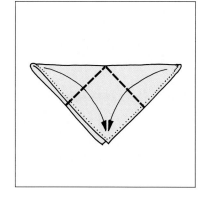

2. Fold the side corners down to the bottom point.

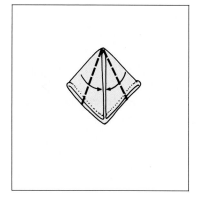

3. Fold the side edges that connect at the top corner inward to meet at the center.

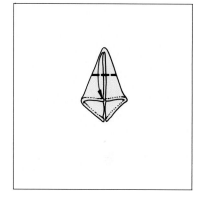

4. Fold the top point down to meet the corners that you folded in the last step.

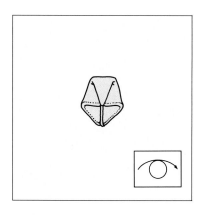

5. Turn the napkin over.

6. Completed Monogram fold.

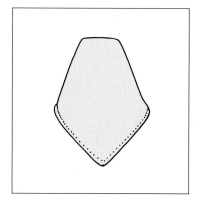

Variation: At step 4, bring the top point down only slightly or not at all. This will give the

napkin a longer shape, more suitable for placement at the side of a plate or under a fork.

The tall, slender shape and deep pocket of this design make it a suitable holder for a flower, breadsticks, straws, chopsticks, or silverware.

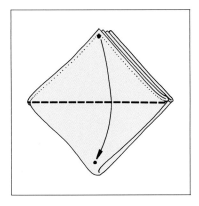 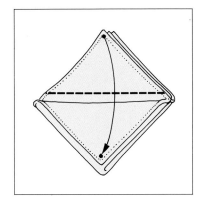 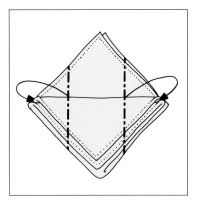 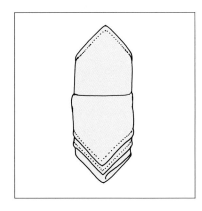

1. Begin with a napkin folded in quarters. Place it on the table so that the four free corners are at the top. Bring the top corner of the first layer down to a little above the bottom corner.

2. Bring the second layer down so that the corner lies a little above the corner of the first layer folded down.

3. Fold the side corners behind to overlap at the back of the napkin. (You may wish to turn the napkin over to make this step easier.)

4. Completed Pointed Pocket.

REVERSIBLE ROLL

(Contributed by Susan Kalish)

This stylish design is most effective when folded from two napkins in contrasting colors. Either lightweight cloth or paper napkins can be used.

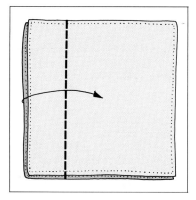

1. Open both napkins and lay one on top of the other. (If you are using a patterned napkin, the wrong sides should face each other.) Fold the left sides of both napkins to the center.

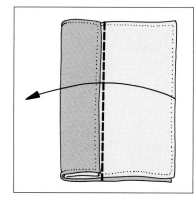

2. Bring both right edges over to the left, folding along the edges that lie at the center of the napkin.

3. Loosely roll both left edges to the right until you have a vertical roll in the center of a rectangle. Flatten the roll to form a band.

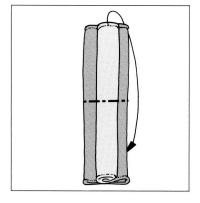

4. Fold the napkin in half, bringing the top edges backward to lie behind the bottom edges.

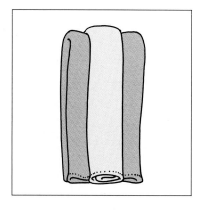

5. Completed Reversible Roll.

Variation: This design also looks attractive folded from a single napkin.

SACHET

Unlike some of the more dramatic folds, it is the intricacy of this design that will impress your guests. The sachet requires a little more practice to fold than some other designs and should be attempted when you have some experience with simpler folds.

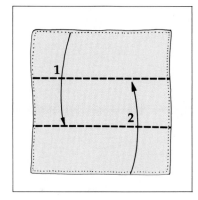

1. Begin with an open napkin. Fold the napkin in thirds, as shown, so the open edge is on top.

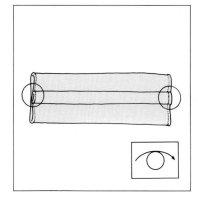

2. Take the first layer of the top edge and fold it down twice to form a narrow band across the center of the napkin.

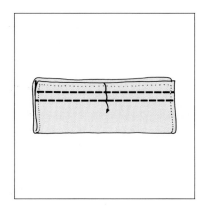

3. Holding the napkin at each side to keep the band in place, carefully turn the napkin over.

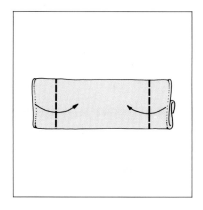

4. Fold the right and left sides inward (approximately one-sixth of the way).

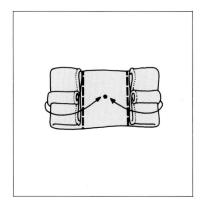

5. Fold in each side to meet at the center.

6. Fold the right side of the napkin backward so that it lies under the left side.

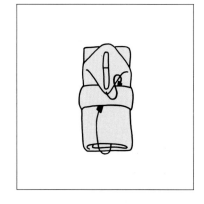

7. Grasp the first layer of the top edge and pull down toward the band. A small diamond shape will form with a slit down its center. Flatten this shape evenly and tuck the bottom point under the band. Repeat at the bottom of your napkin.

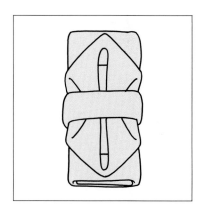

8. Completed Sachet.

*Add an elegant touch to your table with this beautiful
Silk Purse design. Use a large cloth napkin.*

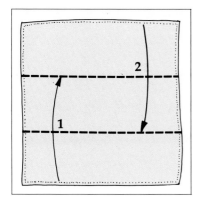

1. Begin with an open, square napkin. Fold the napkin in thirds (as you would fold a letter) so that the open edge is on the bottom.

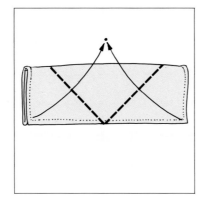

2. Place a finger at the center of the bottom edge and fold up the right and left bottom corners so that both sides of the bottom edge meet at the center.

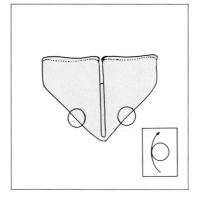

3. Hold the slanted edges of the napkin and flip it over to the other side.

4. Two rectangles extend below the base of a large triangle. Tightly roll each rectangle up as far as you can (just past the base of the triangle).

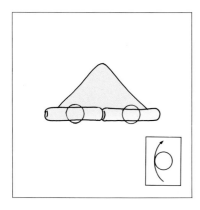

5. While holding the rolls tightly in both hands, flip the napkin over to the other side.

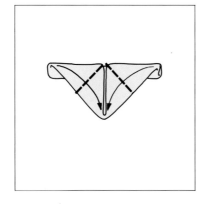

6. Bring the top side corners of the triangle down to the bottom corner.

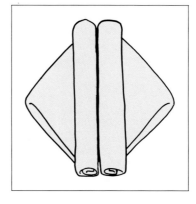

7. Completed Silk Purse. Tighten the rolls if necessary.

Variation: Turn the napkin over after the last step and the design will resemble a mortarboard, an appropriate design for a graduation party.

This design can be made from almost any type of napkin. The deep pocket can be used to hold silverware either at the dining table, the buffet table, or at a picnic. Or make use of the pocket to hold a flower or a favor for each guest.

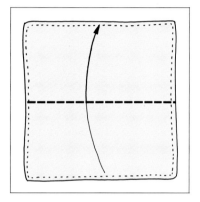

1. Begin with an open napkin. Fold the bottom edge up to the top edge.

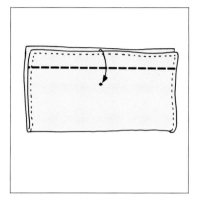

2. There are two layers at the top edge of your napkin. Fold the front layer down to form a hem.

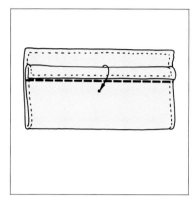

3. Fold the hem down along its bottom edge.

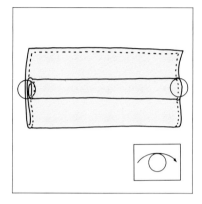

4. You should now have a band running across the center of your napkin. Holding the band in place, turn the napkin over to the back side.

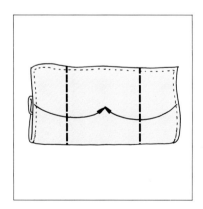

5. Fold the side edges of the napkin in to meet at the center.

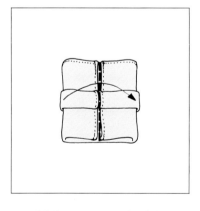

6. Fold the napkin in half down the center.

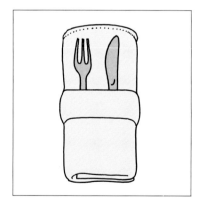

7. Completed Silverware Holder.

This is a fairly simple and versatile fold that can be placed on or beside a plate, in a glass, or slipped through a napkin ring.

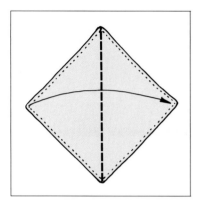

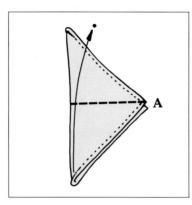

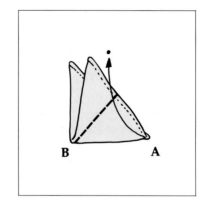

1. Begin with an open, square napkin, turned so that it is shaped like a diamond. Bring the left side corner over to the right side corner.

2. Place one finger at the right side corner (A) and lift the bottom point up on a fold that begins at corner A. Place the bottom point slightly to the right of the top point.

3. Place a finger at the bottom left corner (B) and lift the bottom right point up on a fold that begins at corner B. Place point A slightly to the right of the other two top points.

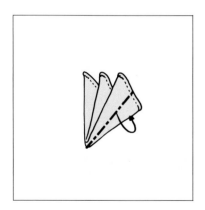

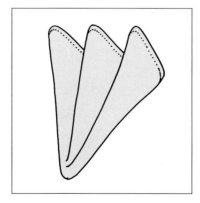

4. Fold the bottom right side backward to give the napkin a more slender form.

5. Completed Slender Points. If you wish to place this fold in a glass, tuck the bottom point under before inserting.

*Leave a flower, lollipop, or other favor poking out of the delightful
Surprise Sack. For a touch of mystery, leave a secret message, fortune,
or candy hidden inside the pocket.*

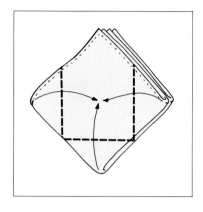

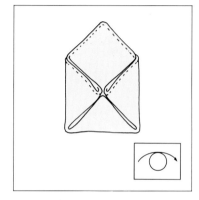

1. Begin with a napkin folded into quarters. Position the napkin so that the four free corners are at the top. Fold the bottom and side corners inward to meet at the center.

2. Turn the napkin over.

3. Fold the first layer of the top corner down.

4. Completed Surprise Sack. Insert a surprise into the pocket.

This design will add elegance to a formal dinner without overpowering the traditional dinnerware or other table decor. If you are using name cards, place the Tri-Fold horizontally on each plate and slip the card behind one of the folded edges. For an extra-special occasion, prepare menu cards listing what will be served and slip them behind the other folded edge.

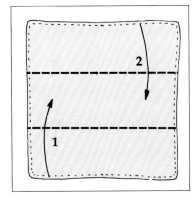

1. Begin with an open napkin. Fold the napkin in thirds, as shown.

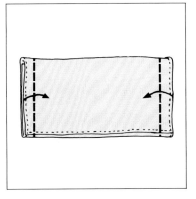

2. Fold in the right and left sides to form a border on each side (approximately two inches [5 cm]) wide.

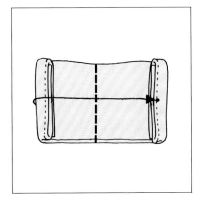

3. Bring the left side over to cover the open edges of the right border.

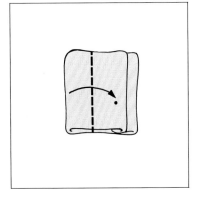

4. Bring the left side toward the right so that each of the folded edges on the right are the same distance apart (see drawing 5).

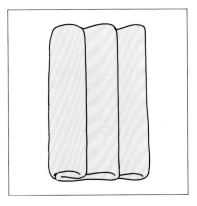

5. The completed Tri-Fold can be placed in a horizontal or vertical position.

Menu
Antipasto

Michael

CHAPTER TWO

Sculptured Designs

The graceful petals of this Bird of Paradise add flair to any table.

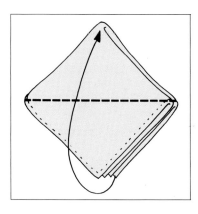

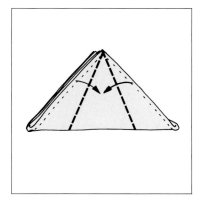

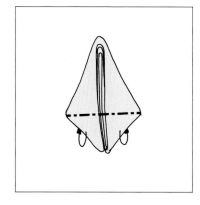

1. Begin with a napkin folded into quarters. Position the napkin so that the four free corners are at the bottom. Fold the bottom corners up to the top.

2. Fold the sides of the triangle in to meet at the center.

3. Fold the bottom points back and upward, to lie behind the rest of the napkin.

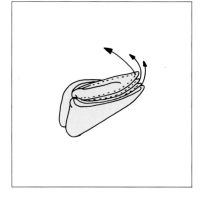

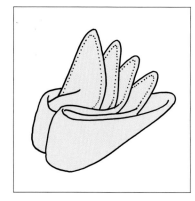

4. Fold the right and left sides of the napkin backward. (If the center opens slightly, leave it that way.)

5. Position the napkin as shown in the drawing and hold tightly at the broad end. At the top edge of the right corner several layers are exposed. One at a time, lift up the first four layers. Leave them staggered and gently curving to form petals.

6. Completed Bird of Paradise. If you have folded the design from a paper napkin, you may wish to insert the broad end of the napkin between the tines of a fork for extra support.

BUTTERFLY

(Design by the author)

Invite spring to your table with this decorative Butterfly design.

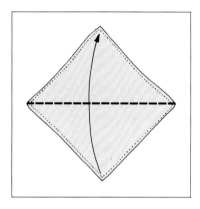

1. Begin with an open, square napkin in the shape of a diamond. Bring the bottom corner up to the top corner.

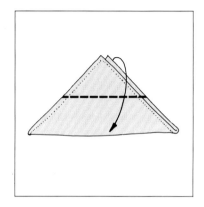

2. Bring the top points down to the center of the bottom edge.

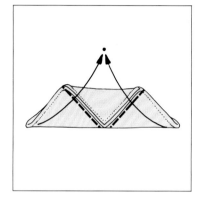

3. Fold both side points up.

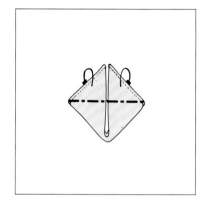

4. Fold the top half of each triangle backward to wrap behind the horizontal folded edge.

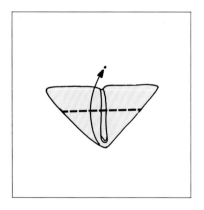

5. Lift up the middle bottom point and position it slightly above the top of the triangle (see drawing 6).

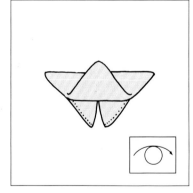

6. Turn the napkin over.

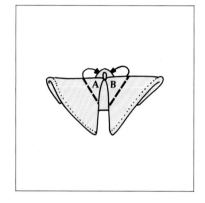

7. Hold the napkin at A and B and push your hands together. The center of the napkin (the body of the butterfly) should raise up and the wings should shift to the position shown in drawing 8.

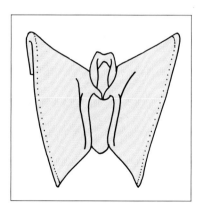

8. Completed Butterfly. If you are using a paper napkin, fold the body over to the right and then to the left to sharpen the creases that separate the body from the wings.

CROWN

The Crown is a classic napkin fold. This stately design can be used to cover and keep warm a roll placed at each place setting, or you can use the top of the Crown as a container for anything you wish.

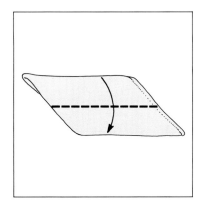

1. Begin with an open napkin. Fold the bottom edge up to the top edge.

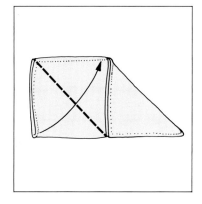

2. Fold the top right corners down to the bottom edge.

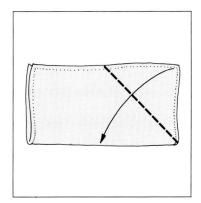

3. Fold the bottom left corner up to the top edge.

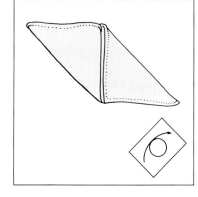

4. Turn the napkin over and position it so that the long folded edges are at the top and bottom.

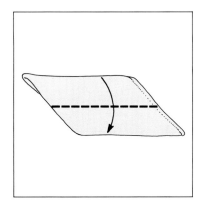

5. Fold the top edge down to the bottom edge.

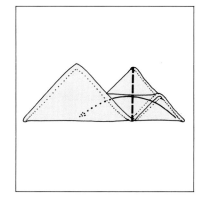

6. Slip a finger under edge A and slide it upward to release the hidden point (see drawing 7).

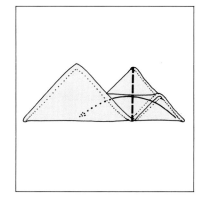

7. Bring the right bottom point over to the left and tuck it under the edge (see drawing 8).

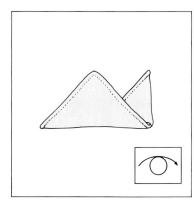

8. Turn the napkin over.

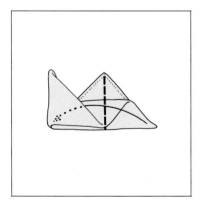

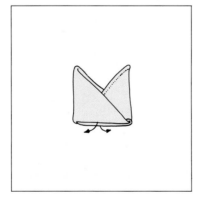

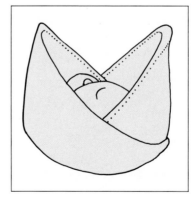

9. Bring the bottom right point over to the left and tuck it into the pocket.

10. Open the Crown at the bottom and pull the edges apart to give it a round shape.

11. Stand the completed Crown on a plate or on the table.

LEAF

(Design by the author)

Celebrate spring or fall with this Leaf design.
The Leaf will stay better if a cloth napkin is used.

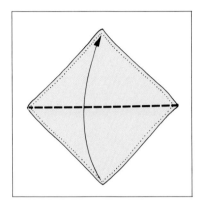

1. Begin with an open, square napkin in the shape of a diamond. Bring the bottom point up to the top point.

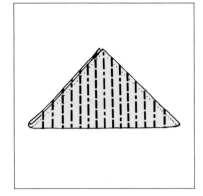

2. Beginning at one side corner, accordion-pleat the napkin across to the opposite corner.

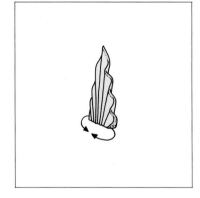

3. Unfold the center pleat. (You may want to count the number of pleats to find the center pleat.)

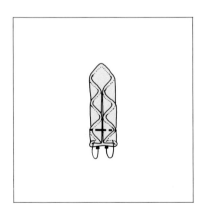

4. Hold the napkin so that the two piles of pleats are lying side by side. Fold back the bottom end of the pleats.

5. Fold the right and left piles of pleats backward to meet behind. (You are refolding on the center pleat.)

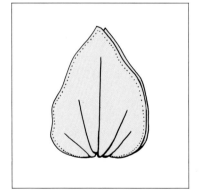

6. Shape the completed Leaf and lay flat on the table or on a plate.

Here's a decorative holder for a paper napkin. If you wish, you can write the name of each guest on the neck of the bird. Laura Kruskal also writes a message on the tail of the bird, so when the napkin is removed, the guest sees the hidden message—"Welcome!" • For each Peacock you will need a small paper napkin (approximately twelve inches [30 cm] square), and a sheet of sturdy paper (approximately eight and a half inches [22 cm] square).

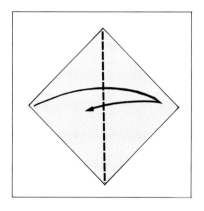

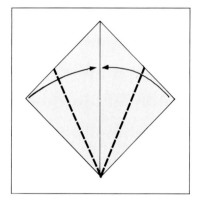

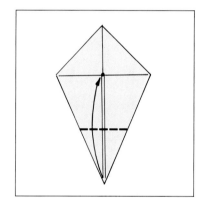

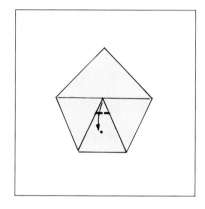

1. Place the sheet of paper on a table so it is in the shape of a diamond. Bring the left side corner over to the right side corner. Crease very hard and unfold.

2. Bring the bottom right edge over to the center crease. Then bring the bottom left edge over to the center crease.

3. Fold the narrow bottom point up to the horizontal edges.

4. Fold the narrow point down a little to form a head.

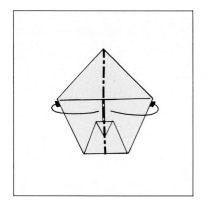

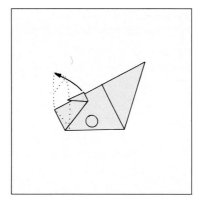

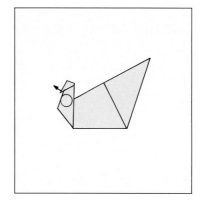

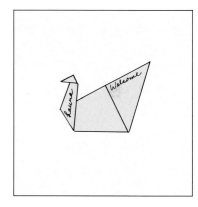

5. Fold the right and left sides backward until they meet.

6. Hold the paper so that the head and the neck are on the top. Grasp the body of the bird (at the circle in the drawing) and pull the neck of the bird away from the body. Pinch the bottom of the neck to lock this position in place.

7. Hold the neck of the bird and with your other hand lift up the head. Pinch where the head and neck connect to lock the head in this position.

8. Stand the bird on a table.

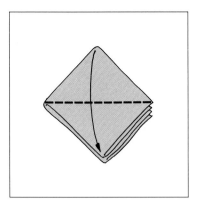 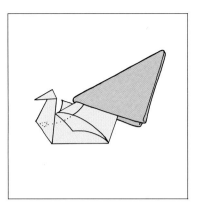 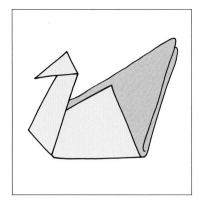

9. Take a paper napkin (folded in quarters) and fold it diagonally in half.

10. Slightly separate the wings of the bird from the body with one hand. With your other hand, lay the napkin over the folded edge at the top of the bird's body. One corner of the napkin should be pointing toward the neck of the bird; the opposite corner should extend past the tail. Let go of the wings you were holding and they will hold the napkin in place.

11. Completed Peacock.

SCALLOP SHELL

This elegant design was inspired by a fan pattern used by
Japanese origami master, Akira Yoshizawa.

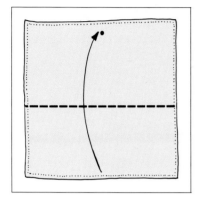

1. Begin with an open napkin. Fold the bottom edge of the napkin up to slightly below the top edge.

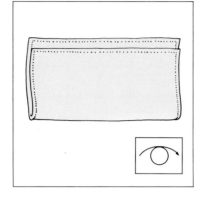

2. Turn the napkin over. The folded edge will remain at the bottom.

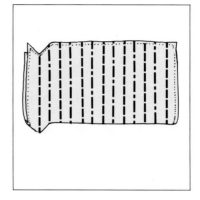

3. Beginning at one side edge, accordion-pleat the napkin across to the opposite side.

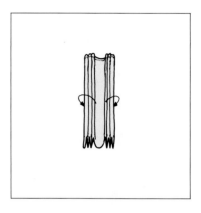

4. Collect half of the pleated edges in one hand and half in the other hand. Spread the two groups apart, as if you were opening a book.

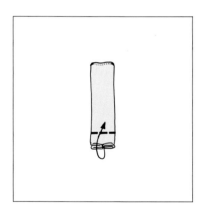

5. Fold the bottom edges up an inch or two (2.5 to 5 cm), folding through all the layers.

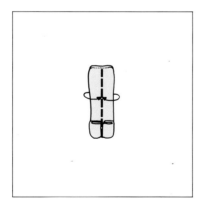

6. Bring the right and left groups of pleats back together again, as if you were closing a book.

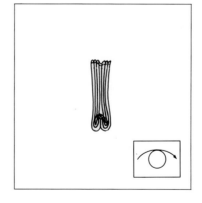

7. Keeping a firm hold at the bottom, turn the napkin over.

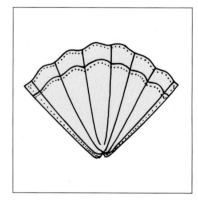

8. Lay the napkin on a plate and spread the pleats apart at the top for your completed Scallop Shell.

STANDING FAN

Often seen in restaurants or cruise ships, this dressy fan design is always appealing.
Use a sturdy napkin that will hold its shape; cloth is best.

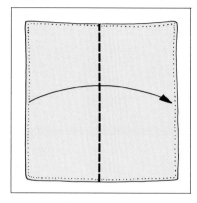

1. Begin with an open napkin. Fold the napkin in half, from left to right.

2. Beginning at the bottom edge, accordion-pleat two-thirds of the way toward the top edge.

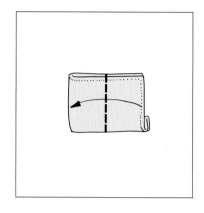

3. The pleats you just made should be behind the bottom edge. Fold the napkin in half from right to left; the pleats should now be on the outside.

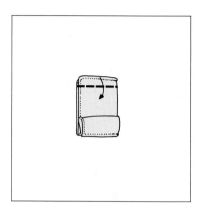

4. Fold the top edge of the napkin down to form a small hem.

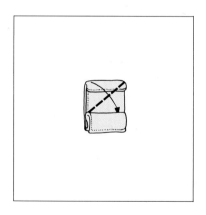

5. Fold the left side of the napkin down diagonally and tuck it behind the pleats. (If this edge does not fit neatly behind the pleats, go back to step 4 and adjust the size of the hem you made.)

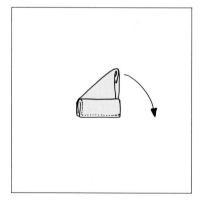

6. Stand the napkin on the right edge.

7. Release the fan.

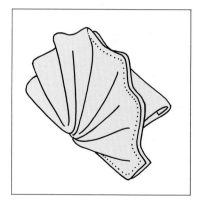

8. Completed Standing Fan.

This delightful Swan should be folded from a square paper napkin. For best results make sharp creases. This fold may take a little practice to perfect.

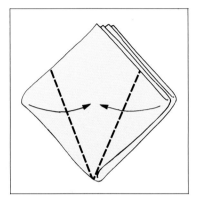

1. Begin with a napkin folded into quarters. Position the napkin so that the four free corners are at the top. Fold the bottom side edges in to meet at center.

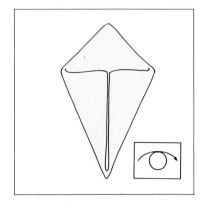

2. Turn the napkin over, keeping the sharp point at the bottom.

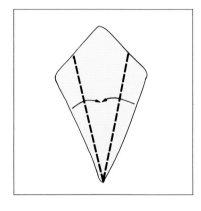

3. Narrow the sharp point by folding the long sides in to meet at the center.

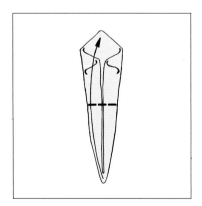

4. Fold the bottom point up to the top point.

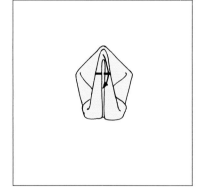

5. Fold the sharp point down a little to form the head.

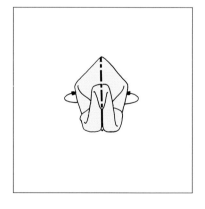

6. Fold the napkin in half along the center line so that the right and left sides go backward. (The head will remain on the outside.)

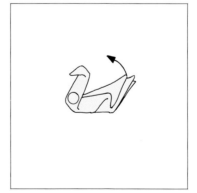

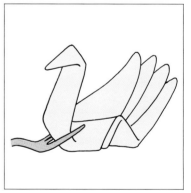

7. Rotate the napkin to the position shown and hold it at the circle. With your other hand lift the neck slightly and pinch it near the base to lock it in place.

8. Hold the neck at the circle. With your other hand lift the head away from the neck and pinch it in place where the head and neck connect.

9. Hold the swan at the base of the neck. There should be several layers of paper at the tail end of the swan. Carefully pull up each individual layer and separate them slightly to form a "fluffy" tail.

10. To keep the swan from spreading apart, insert the tines of a fork into the front end of the swan (at the base of the neck), or tie a thin piece of ribbon around the neck.

The layers of petals and lovely flower shape make the Water Lily a traditional favorite. Use it as is to adorn your table, or as a container to hold a roll, a small crock of soup, or even nuts. This design will work best if folded from a stiff napkin.

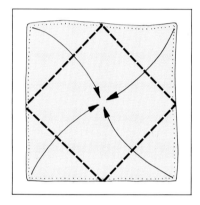 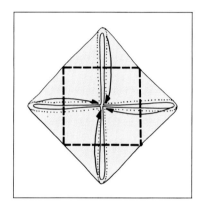 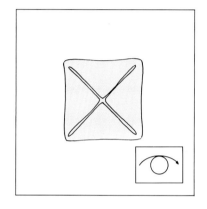 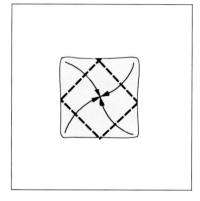

1. Begin with an open, square napkin. Bring all four corners inward to meet at the center.

2. Fold each outside corner in to meet at the center.

3. While you hold the center points in place with one hand, slip your other hand underneath the napkin and carefully flip it over to the back.

4. Fold each outside corner in to the center.

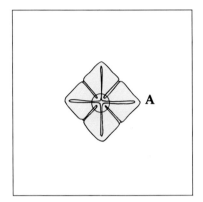 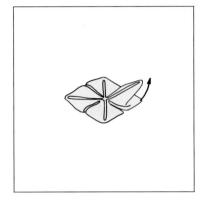  

5. While doing this next step, it is very important that you keep the center points you just folded securely in place, either by holding them down with your hand or by placing a glass on top of them. Starting at one outside corner (A), slip your free hand underneath the napkin and pull out one of the loose corners from the underside of the napkin.

Pull this corner out and upward so that it softly wraps itself around corner A to form the shape of a petal (see drawing 6).

6. Repeat step 5 on the other three corners. Remember to keep the center points firmly in place.

7. Slip your hand under side B and pull out the loose corner from under the napkin. Pull the corner upward and tug at it gently.

8. Repeat step 7 on the three remaining corners from the underside of the napkin. If your napkin is stiff enough, it will form a soft cup shape.

9. Completed Water Lily.

Variation: If you are using a very large or limp napkin, you may wish to add an extra layer of petals to your flower. Repeat step 2 before turning the napkin over at step 3. After step 8 there will be four more loose corners underneath that can be pulled out and upward. Your finished flower will be smaller and will hold its shape better.

WINGS

(Design by the author)

Wings is a dramatic design. At the last step, it can be slightly varied to resemble a bird, a dragonfly, or a butterfly. Use a cloth napkin or a large paper napkin.

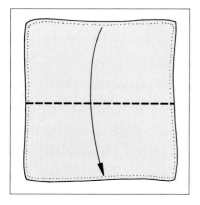

1. Begin with an open, square napkin. Bring the top edge down to the bottom edge.

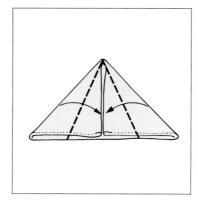

2. Bring both top corners down to meet at the center of the bottom edge.

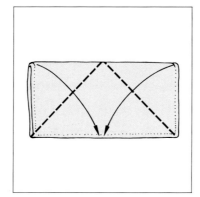

3. Fold the slanted sides in to meet at the center.

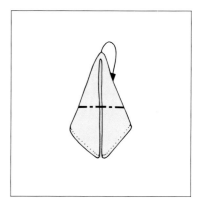

4. Fold the top point backward to meet the two points already at the bottom.

5. Push the right and left sides backward until they meet.

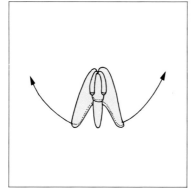

6. While leaving the center fold in place, grasp the right and left bottom points and raise them up as far as they will go.

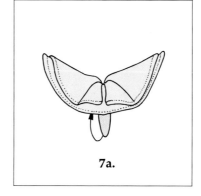

7a.

7b.

7. You can leave the bottom point where it is to resemble a dragonfly (see drawing 7a), or fold it behind for finished wings (see drawing 7b).

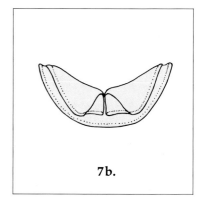

Note: When using a large paper napkin, this design seems to work better when the bottom point is left down. With a cloth napkin, you may wish to fold the bottom point behind.

CHAPTER THREE

*Designs to Use With a
Napkin Ring or a Glass*

© Tony Cenicola

BOUQUET

*Create the illusion of a bouquet of flowers at every place setting
with this very simple napkin fold and a napkin ring.*

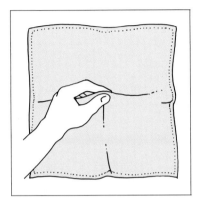 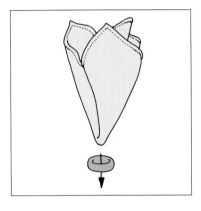 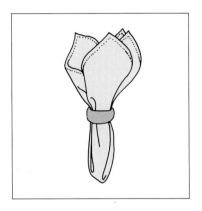 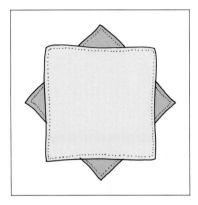

1. Begin with an open napkin. Hold the very center of the napkin and lift it in the air, letting the rest of the napkin hang loosely in soft folds.

2. Slip the closed end of the napkin you are holding in your hand into a napkin ring and slide the ring down a few inches.

3. Shape the napkin for a pretty Bouquet.

Variation: For a fuller and more colorful Bouquet, start with two napkins placed one on top of the other.

BOWTIE

This smart-looking fold will dress up your table for any occasion.

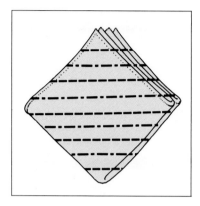 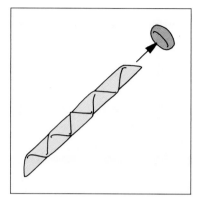 

1. Begin with a napkin folded into quarters. Starting at one corner, accordion-pleat to the opposite corner.

2. While holding the pleats together in one hand, slip the napkin into a napkin ring and slide the ring to the center.

3. Fan out the sides to show off the completed Bowtie.

Variation: Vary the position of the napkin ring for a different effect.

CACTUS
(Design by Susan Kalish)

The graceful leaves of this design add style to any table setting.
Use a cloth napkin and a napkin ring with a wide opening.

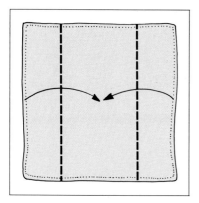

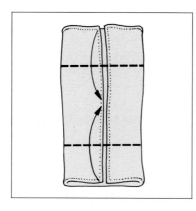

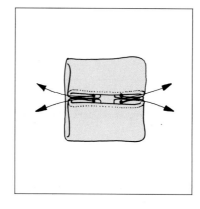

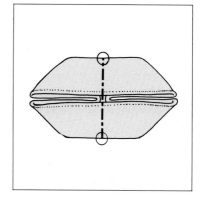

1. Begin with an open, square napkin. Fold the right and left sides in to meet at the center.

2. Fold the top and bottom edges in to meet at the center.

3. Look under the layers where the edges meet at the center: You will see four loose corners. One at a time, pull each corner out to the side. Each corner will form a point, as shown in drawing 4.

4. Lift the napkin at the center of the top and bottom edges and let the points hang down so that it folds in half backward. Lay the napkin back on the table and turn it so that all the points are at the top.

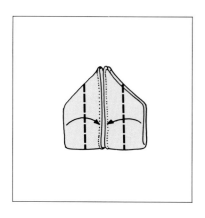

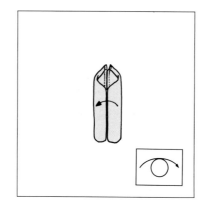

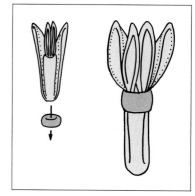

5. Fold the side edges in to meet at the center.

6. Narrow the napkin again by folding the side edges to the center.

7. Fold the napkin in half and turn it over.

8. Insert the bottom end into a napkin ring and push the ring up a few inches, then shape the leaves of the Cactus.

*This festive fold is made from two different colored napkins. You can
match the colors to go with a specific holiday theme, or just pick two colors that
look good together. Paper napkins are fine for this design.*

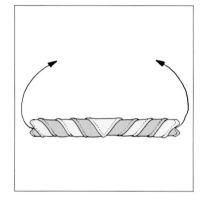

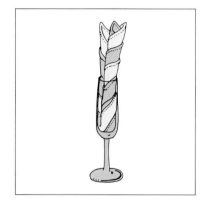

1. Place one open napkin over the other. The top napkin should be slightly higher, creating a V-shaped border approximately one inch (2.5 cm) wide.

2. Beginning at the bottom corner, roll both napkins together toward the top corner.

3. Your roll should have a striped design similar to a candy cane. Bring the opposite ends of the roll together, loosely folding the roll in half.

4. Insert the folded edge of the roll into a glass.

FAN

In Japan, the spreading fan is regarded as a symbol of growing prosperity and good fortune ahead. It is frequently depicted in their decorative arts and used for celebratory occasions. For variety, place the fold in a tall glass instead of in a napkin ring.

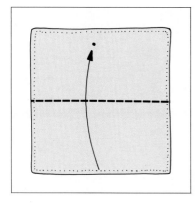

1. Begin with an open napkin. Fold the bottom edge up so that it lies slightly below the top edge. (Note: If you are using a napkin with a printed pattern, fold the bottom edge all the way to the top edge.)

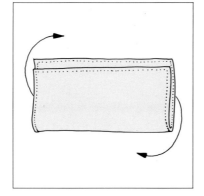

2. Rotate the napkin so that the side edges become the top and bottom edges.

3. Beginning at the bottom edge, accordion-pleat the napkin up to the top edge.

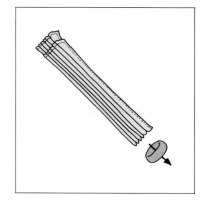

4. Insert a napkin ring onto the right end of the napkin. The napkin ring can be left near the bottom of the pleated napkin, or you can slide it furthur up, depending on how much you would like your fan to spread.

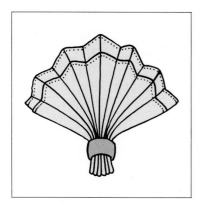

5. Place the napkin on a plate and spread the top pleats to form a Fan.

I R I S

The Iris design can be grand or dainty, depending on the size and type of napkin used.

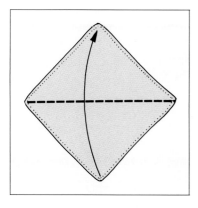

1. Begin with an open, square napkin placed on the table in the shape of a diamond. Fold the bottom point up to the top point.

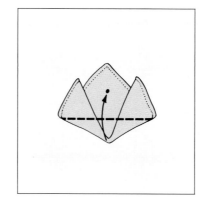

2. Hold your finger at the center of the bottom edge as you fold up the left and right points so that they are at the same height as, but slightly to the sides of, the center point (see drawing 3).

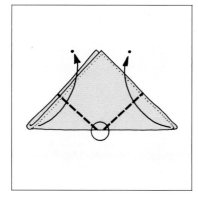

3. Fold the bottom point up as shown.

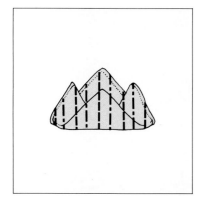

4. Beginning at one side, accordion-pleat the napkin across to the opposite side.

5. Place the base of the napkin in a glass (if the napkin is cloth) or insert between the tines of a fork (if the napkin is paper). Spread out the sides to form petals.

With this fold you can put a flower at every place setting without running out to the florist!

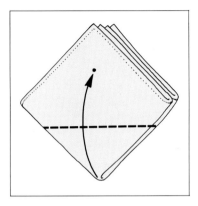

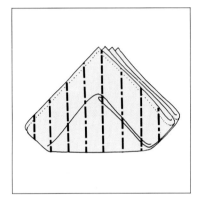

1. Begin with a napkin folded into quarters. Position the napkin so that the four free corners are at the top. Fold the bottom corner about one-third of the way up.

2. Starting at one side corner, accordion-pleat the napkin to the opposite side corner.

3. Insert the bottom of the napkin into a glass or ring. You should have four loose points at the top of the napkin. Separate the four layers.

4. Shape the petals of your finished flower.

Variation: When using paper napkins, try using two different colors and folding them as one. First unfold each napkin completely and place one directly over the other. Refold them in quarters and continue from step 1.

ROSETTE

*The Rosette is a very showy design, especially when made
from brightly colored napkins.*

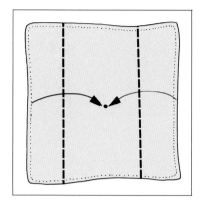

1. Begin with an open napkin. Fold the right and left sides in to meet at the center.

2. Starting at the bottom edge, accordion-pleat the napkin up to the top edge.

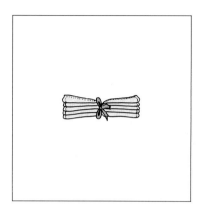

3. Tie a narrow ribbon around the center of the napkin (or use a very narrow ring). Lay the fan on a plate and let the pleats fan out into a full circle.

4. Completed Rosette.

Let the soft folds of this pleated design spread out to form
a frilly edge resembling ruffles.

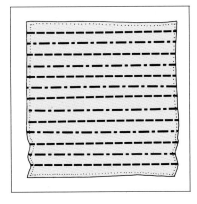 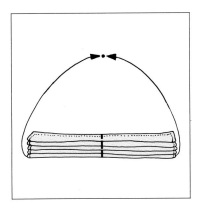 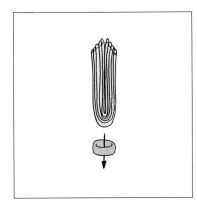 

1. Begin with an open napkin. Starting at the bottom edge, accordion-pleat the napkin up to the top edge.

2. Bring the right and left ends of the napkin together, folding it in half.

3. Slip the folded end of the napkin through a ring. Slide the ring almost halfway up the length of the napkin and spread the end of the top edges down to the left and right, forming a circular shape.

4. Completed Ruffles.

SCARF

(Design by Laura Kruskal)

*This pretty shape will adapt to the napkin you choose, whether
it is vividly colored or delicately lacy.*

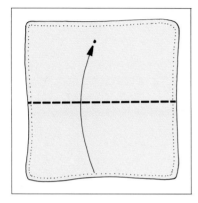

1. Begin with an open napkin. Fold the bottom edge up to slightly below the top edge.

2. Turn the napkin over so that the folded edge remains at the bottom.

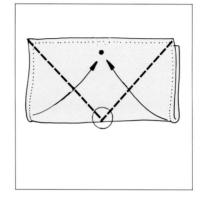

3. Place a finger at the center of the bottom edge and fold the right and left bottom corners up to meet at the center.

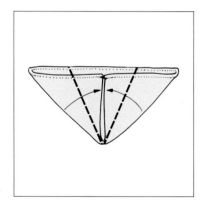

4. Fold the slanted side edges in to meet at the center.

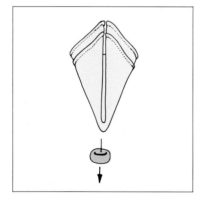

5. Slip the bottom point through a napkin ring.

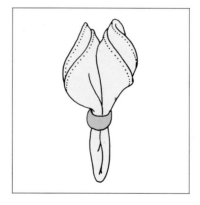

6. Completed Scarf.

Variation: This design is also very attractive when laid flat, without a ring.

CHAPTER FOUR

Table Service Designs

Aside from crackers, this clever basket can also be used to serve wrapped candies, packets of sugar, or other small table fare. A cloth napkin is required for this fold. This is not an easy fold and may take several attempts to perfect.

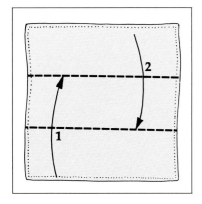 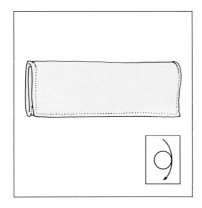 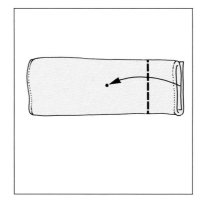 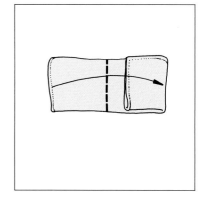

1. Begin with an open napkin. Fold the napkin in thirds, as you would fold a letter.

2. Turn the napkin over.

3. Fold the right side edge to the center. (This is a temporary fold that serves as a guide for the next step. It is unfolded in step 5.)

4. Bring the left edge to the far right edge.

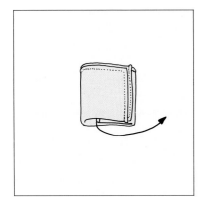 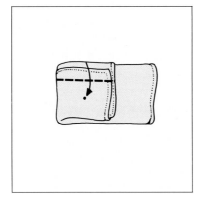 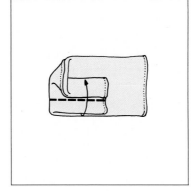 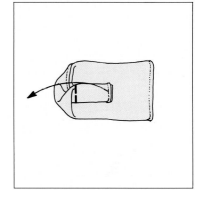

5. Reach under the flap you just folded over and unfold the flap you folded over in step 3.

6. Lift the top edge of the flap and fold it down one-third of the way. As you do this, the top left corner will squash down and form a small triangle (see drawing 7).

7. Repeat step 6 at the bottom of the flap.

8. You now have a narrow flap extending from two small triangles. At the base of the triangles, fold the flap over to the left.

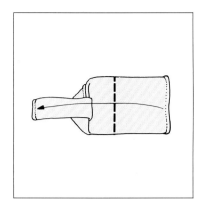 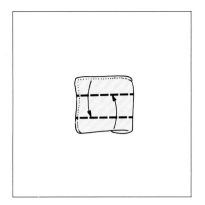 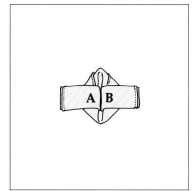 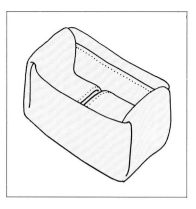

9. Fold the right edge over to the left edge of the narrowed flap.

10. Repeat steps 6 to 8 on the right side.

11. Hold at edges A and B and turn the napkin inside out. The flaps that are now extending out to the sides will fall inside and line a rectangular-shape basket.

12. Completed Cracker Holder. Shape the basket by pressing your fingers into the bottom corners and straightening the sides and lining.

HOT STUFF

(Adapted by the author)

This simple fold turns a single-layered napkin into a compact, multilayered pocket. Use it as a pot holder or as a trivet. It is suitable for use with hot dishes, but should not be used for things taken directly from the oven. Fold from a heavy cloth napkin. If you are using a napkin with a printed pattern, begin with the patterned side facing up.

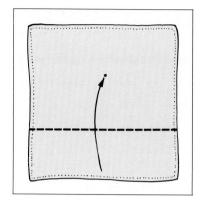

1. Begin with an open, square napkin. Fold the bottom edge one-third of the way up.

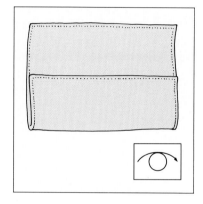

2. Turn the napkin over.

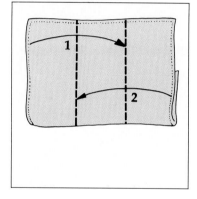

3. Fold the napkin in thirds, as shown.

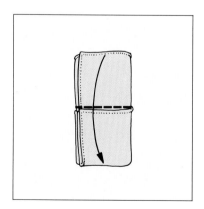

4. Fold the top edges down to the bottom.

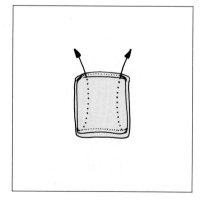

5. At the top edge of the napkin is a pocket. Insert your hands into the right and left sides of the pocket, leaving your thumbs on the outside. Turn the napkin inside out (like a glove).

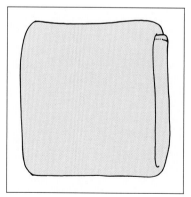

6. Neaten the corners of the pouch by poking your fingers down to the bottom corners and your pot holder or hot plate is complete.

Here's a design you can use as a placemat when folded from a large cloth napkin. As with Hot Stuff, if you are using a napkin with a pattern, make sure the patterned side is facing up.

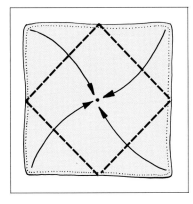

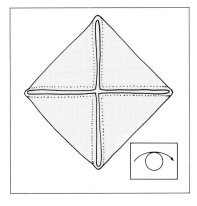

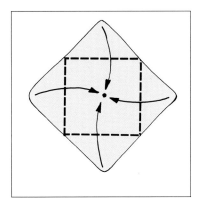

1. Begin with an open, square napkin. Bring all four corners in to meet at the center.

2. Hold down the center points with one hand, and carefully turn the napkin over.

3. Bring all four outside corners in to meet at the center.

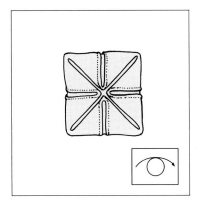

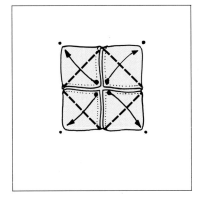

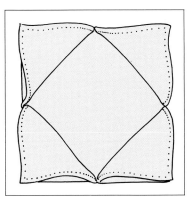

4. Carefully turn the napkin over.

5. Take one of the inside corners and fold it out to the nearest outside corner. Tug at it slightly to help keep it in place. Repeat with the other three inside corners.

6. Your completed Placemat will probably fit well under a small luncheon plate.

LEARNING NAPKIN FOLDS

For anyone with little or no experience in napkin folding, the secret to success is patience and practice. Start out with a simple fold and try it when you have enough time to read the directions carefully (not five minutes before your dinner party). If you get stuck at a particular step, look ahead to the next drawing to see the form you are trying to create. You may wish to practice a new fold on a paper napkin before attempting it on a freshly ironed and starched cloth napkin.

Since the same napkin fold is used several times when setting the table, after the first two napkins try to see if you can remember the folding sequence without using the directions. Teaching the fold to a friend, a child, or a guest at your table will also help you to remember the folding sequence the next time you try it. After you have successfully mastered some of the simpler folds, give one of the more difficult folds a try.

What happens when you are visiting a friend or relative who was so impressed with the beautifully folded napkins at your house, that they now ask if you would "dress up" their table setting, and you don't have the folding directions on hand? Well, I usually do one of three things. One is to improvise. Many new and charming designs can be created if you just experiment. The second option is to fold one of the classic napkin fold designs that are done so many times that you remember them by heart. The third choice is to recall the folding pattern from a napkin story.

NAPKIN STORIES

As you are learning a new napkin fold from the instructions, you may find that you associate some of the shapes formed along the way with familiar objects (e.g., a book, box, house, kite, etc.). By remembering these associations or even making up simple stories to go with them, you will find that the next time you try to fold the same pattern you may not need to refer back to the directions. If your story is particularly clever, you may even want to use it to entertain children. Here is an example of a simple story I made up to go with the folding sequence of the Wings napkin fold found on page 82.

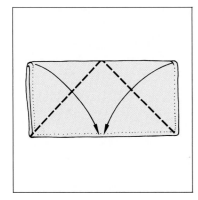

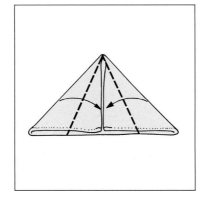

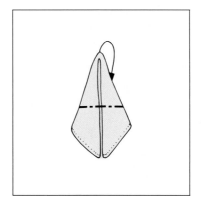

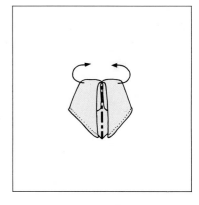

One day a bird was flying through the sky looking for a place to make a nest. When she looked down, she spotted a large building, but it was still under construction and it didn't have a roof yet. So the bird kept looking.

Then she saw a house with a slanted roof. "That's no good," thought the bird. "My nest would slide right down the sides of that roof." So she kept looking.

The next building she passed had a tall, pointed spire on top. "I certainly can't make my nest there," thought the bird.

But the next roof she flew by was flat on top. "This is perfect," thought the bird.

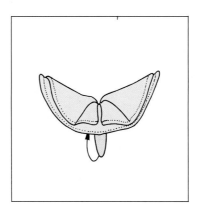

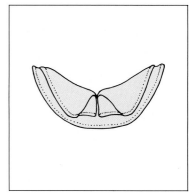

So she spread out her wings…

…and tucked in her feet and was happy to finally have found a home.

CREATIVE IDEAS WITH NAPKIN FOLDS

DOUBLE NAPKINS

Folding two napkins at once is no more work than folding one, and by placing two napkins of different colors, either directly on top of the other or one shifted slightly to the side, you can create some very dramatic results.

NAPKIN RINGS

Napkin rings serve the dual purpose of holding a napkin in a certain form or design and decorating your table. In some homes, cloth napkins were placed in personalized napkin rings after a meal so that each family member would then be able to keep track of their napkin for the next meal. • Store-bought napkin rings offer convenience and can be very attractive. You may choose to "custom design" your own napkin rings to coordinate with your table setting. Here are some ideas for creating your own decorative napkin rings.

RIBBON

Check out the notions department of a fabric or department store for ribbons and other fabric trimmings. Choose a simple satin ribbon, lace trim, or a ribbon streaked with gold thread, depending on the effect you wish to create. For your napkin ring, simply tie the ribbon around the napkin and into a bow. Or, create a bow or other fanciful design from your trim and attach each to a small piece of elastic, either tied or sewed into a loop.

For a very special look, braid three different colored ribbons together and then wrap them around the napkin. Tie each color ribbon into a separate bow, or tie all the ends into one knot and let them hang freely like streamers.

HOLIDAY TRIMMINGS

Frilly silver and gold trim used to decorate at Christmastime will create a festive look when tied around your napkins. Plastic beads usually strung on Christmas trees can also be formed into a loop and wound around a napkin. Experiment with other types of holiday and package trims, paper or silk flowers, etc. These can be attached to ribbon or elastic, which can easily be wrapped around your napkin.

PIPE CLEANERS

Colorful pipe cleaners can be used singly or in groups of matching colors to create fun and inexpensive napkin rings. Wind the center of a pipe cleaner around a cardboard tube (such as an empty tube from a roll of paper towels). Twist the ends together and then wind each loose end around a pencil to shape it like a spring, or form the ends into any design you wish.

PAPER RING/NAME CARD

Here's an idea for making a simple napkin ring that also serves as a name card. It is made from a strip of paper and will work best when used with paper napkins.

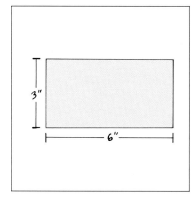

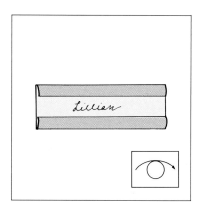

1. Start with a strip (approximately six inches by three inches [15 cm by 8 cm]) of colored or foil wrapping paper that is white on the reverse side.

2. Looking at the white side of your strip, write a message or the name of your guest near the center of the strip. Then fold in a small hem (approximately one-half inch [1 cm]) on both long sides of the strip.

3. Turn the strip over to the colored side.

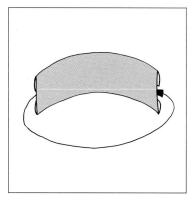

4. Bring both short ends together and slip one inside the other. Let the ends overlap approximately one and a half inches (4 cm).

5. Turn the ring over so that the writing shows and slip a paper napkin through the ring.

CARDBOARD TUBE NAPKIN RING

Save the cardboard tubes from paper towels and toilet paper rolls to make your own unique napkin rings to coordinate with your napkins and table setting. For each napkin holder, cut a ring from the tube approximately three-quarters of an inch to one and a quarter inches (2 to 3 cm) wide. This can be done with a matte knife or a single-edge razor blade. Then decorate the ring as you wish. Here are some suggestions:

Fabric

Cut a small rectangle of fabric long enough to cover the outside of the ring, and wide enough so that the edges can be folded in to cover the inside. Form a small hem at one short end of the material and glue it in place using white glue. Glue the short raw edge to the cardboard ring, then wrap the material around the ring so that the short end with the hem over-laps the short raw edge. Glue the hem end in place. Apply glue to the top edge of the material that overhangs the edge of the cardboard ring. Fold the top edge of the fabric inside the ring, and hold it in place until the fabric sticks to the cardboard tube. Repeat on the bottom edge of the fabric for your finished napkin ring. Thin fabrics are easier to work with; choose a color or pattern that coordinates with your napkins and dinnerware. This technique can be used with pieces of wallpaper to cover cardboard rings.

Papier-mâché

You can create a variety of hand-designed napkin rings using a cardboard tube covered with papier-mâché and then decorated. Use your own recipe for papier-mâché or try the following method:

Materials:
cardboard tubes
1/2 c. water
1/4 c. flour
all-purpose white glue
paper scraps (computer paper, typing paper, stationery, tissue paper, etc.)
sheet of aluminum foil
tempera or acrylic paint
acrylic spray or varnish

1. Cut the cardboard tube into rings as described above.
2. Prepare paper scraps: Take sheets of new or discarded paper and tear them into small pieces approximately 1/2 inch by 2 1/2 inches (1.5 cm by 6.5 cm).
3. Cover the work area with old newspapers.
4. Prepare a flour paste: Put the water in a bowl or container (preferably one you can throw away after using). As you stir, gradually add the flour and mix to a smooth consistency. Add a squirt of white glue and blend it into the mixture.
5. Dip each scrap individually into the flour paste and squeeze out any excess paste by pulling the scrap through your fingers. Apply the paper scraps to your cardboard ring by overlapping each piece slightly with the

pieces already applied. After you have applied one or two layers, let the ring dry on a sheet of aluminum foil. When slightly dry, you may wish to apply additional layers until the band is the thickness you desire.

6. To decorate: Use tissue paper or other colorful scraps dipped in the flour paste as your outside layer, or after the papier-mâché is completely dry (let it dry at least twenty-four hours), decorate it with acrylic or tempera paints.

7. To protect: Spray each ring with several coats of clear acrylic spray or apply a coat of acrylic varnish with a brush.

Cord

Decorate your napkin rings by wrapping them with ribbon, jute, twine, raffia, or cord bought from a notions store. Leave several inches loose before you begin wrapping the rings and tie the two loose ends together when you are finished, hiding the knot.

PICTURE INDEX

This index will help you select the best napkin fold for any occasion. Just choose the design you want by looking at the finished result here, then turn to the corresponding page for folding instructions.

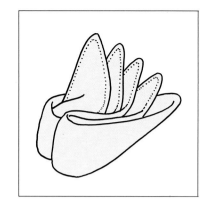

Bird of Paradise
page 61

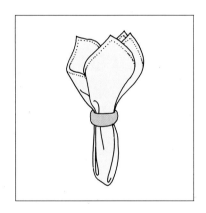

Bouquet
page 87

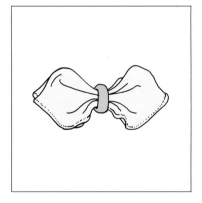

Bowtie
page 89

Breeze
page 16

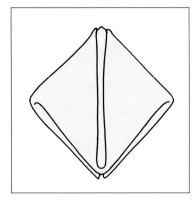

Bun Warmer
page 18

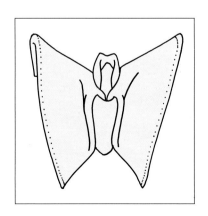

Butterfly
page 62

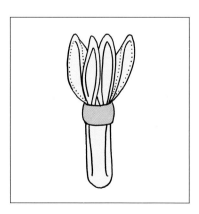

Cactus
page 91

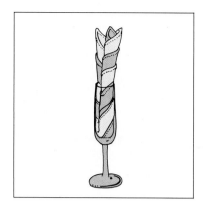

Candy Cane
page 92

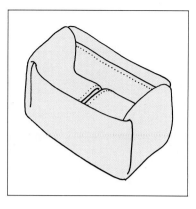

Cracker Holder
page 108

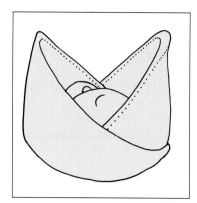

Crown
page 64

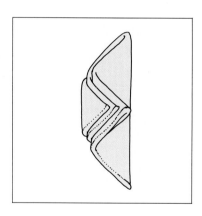

Deco
page 21

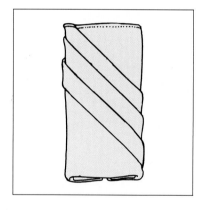

Diagonal Stripes
page 22

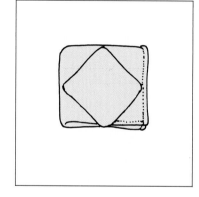

Diamond in the Square
page 25

Double Flap Purse
page 27

Emperor's Robe
page 29

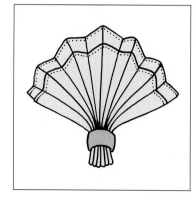

Fan
page 95

Haori
page 30

Hers
page 32

His
page 35

Hot Stuff
page 113

Iris
page 97

Kimono
page 37

Leaf
page 67

Monogram Fold
page 41

Peacock
page 68

Petals
page 98

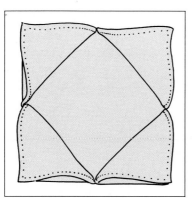

Placemat
page 114

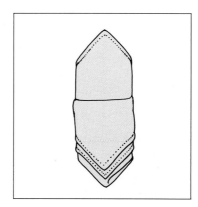

Pointed Pocket
page 42

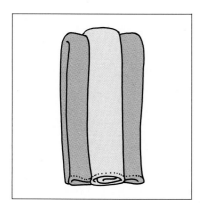

Reversible Roll
page 44

Rosette
page 100

Ruffles
page 102

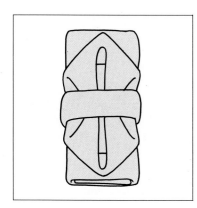

Sachet
page 47

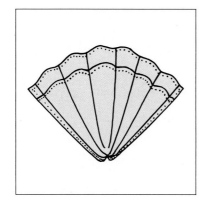

Scallop Shell
page 73

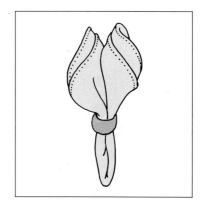

Scarf
page 105

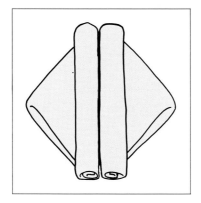

Silk Purse
page 49

Silverware Holder
page 50

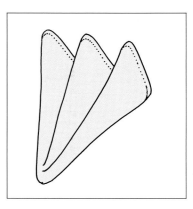

Slender Points
page 53

Standing Fan
page 75

Surprise Sack
page 54

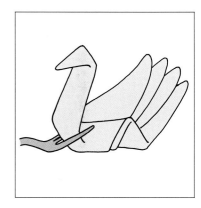

Swan
page 76

Tri-Fold
page 56

Water Lily
page 78

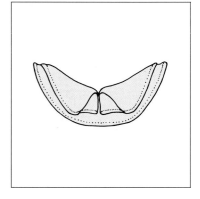

Wings
page 82